Tell Your Parents

GREEN
CHANGES
You Can Make
Around Your Home

WITHDRAWN

Carol Parenzan Smalley

Mitchell Lane
PUBLISHERS
P.O. Box 196
Hockessin, Delaware 19707
Visit us on the web: www.mitchelllane.com
Comments? email us: mitchelllane@mitchelllane.com

Mitchell Lane
PUBLISHERS

Tell Your Parents

All About Electric and Hybrid Cars
Green Changes You Can Make Around Your Home
How to Harness Solar Power for Your Home
How to Use Wind Power to Light and Heat Your Home
How You Can Use Waste Energy to Heat
and Light Your Home

Copyright © 2010 by Mitchell Lane Publishers

All rights reserved. No part of this book may be reproduced without written permission from the publisher. Printed and bound in the United States of America.

PUBLISHER'S NOTE: The facts on which the story in this book is based have been thoroughly researched. Documentation of such research can be found on page 44. While every possible effort has been made to ensure accuracy, the publisher will not assume liability for damages caused by inaccuracies in the data, and makes no warranty on the accuracy of the information contained herein.

Excerpt from "Power from Above" used with permission. Special thanks to David Chameides and Jonathan Alcorn for allowing us to use their photographs.

Printing 1 2 3 4 5 6 7 8 9

**Library of Congress
Cataloging-in-Publication Data**

Smalley, Carol Parenzan, 1960–
  Green changes you can make around your home / by Carol Parenzan Smalley.
    p. cm. — (Tell your parents)
  Includes bibliographical references and index.
  ISBN 978-1-58415-764-9 (library bound)
  1. Environmental protection—Citizen participation—Juvenile literature.
  2. Sustainable living—Juvenile literature.
  3. Environmentalism—Juvenile literature. I. Title.
  TD171.7.S63 2010
  640—dc22
                                                    2009004527

                                                    PLB

CONTENTS

Words in **bold** type can be found in the glossary.

Zac Efron

Bindi Irwin

IT'S ~~NOT~~ EASY BEING GREEN

Bindi Irwin was only nine years old when she decided to make a difference. She is the daughter of the late Crocodile Hunter, Steve Irwin, and Terri Irwin, owner of Australia Zoo. Through their wildlife conservation efforts, her parents taught her the importance of **green living**.

Green living is a lifestyle. People who embrace this lifestyle want to have as little impact as possible on the earth and its natural resources. They want to *reduce* the amount of natural resources they use, including water, wood, and **fossil fuels**; to *reuse* items that have not reached the end of their life; and to *recycle* things that are made of useful ingredients, such as cotton, plastic, or metal. They also want to be sure that their actions do not pollute the planet

through trash or toxic chemicals. Green living can involve changes in a person's choice of transportation; the food that he or she eats; his or her consumption, or use, of electricity; and even the trash he or she generates or leaves behind. Green living is sometimes called **sustainable living**.

Bindi created Bindi Wear International, a clothing line that features **eco-friendly** T-shirts, sweaters, swimwear, sleepwear, hats, and bags. Bindi Wear shoes are made from recycled rubber. One hundred percent of the profits from Bindi's eco-efforts go to help Australia Zoo's conservation programs.

Bindi is not the only young person thinking green. *High School Musical* star Zac Efron arrived in an eco-

limousine for the 2007 Teen Choice Awards. Miley Cyrus, known to many as Hannah Montana, chooses not to eat meat. Her vegetarian lifestyle places less stress on the planet. Instead of riding in a car, she sometimes rides her bicycle around the set of her show. There's a new nickname sprouting to describe today's teenager: GTG, which stands for *Gen-Teen Greenies*.

New York green thinkers ages 7 to 21 are becoming **eco-entrepreneurs**. They combine food, farming, and small business skills as they grow and sell fruit and vegetables in their area. The Green Teen, which is part of Cornell University's Cooperative Extension program, mans booths at local farmers markets. They also make and sell their own salsa—Green Teen's Official Fantastico Down and Dirty Salsa.

In California, green teens run a program called Food from the 'Hood. Started in 1992, this local group has made a global impact. The teens grow produce for local food banks and for markets, and they make and sell salad dressing. The program has helped local food banks, and part of the profit is used to send student-managers to college.

Nineteen-year-old Alyse Lui remembers when her family was nicknamed the French Fry Family. The Lui vehicle runs on **biodiesel** made from used vegetable oil from restaurants. "I thought it was amusing," said Alyse. "We could tell where we had gotten our oil by the smell of the car when it was running. Sometimes it really did smell like french fries, sometimes more like Chinese food.

"My family's approach had a big impact on me in general, though I never really realized it until recently," explained the Northern California teen. Her family has always been environmentally conscious. They recycle and use energy-efficient lightbulbs and appliances. They installed outdoor solar lights and planned to create a water collection system to help meet the water needs of their horses on their mountain property. "We've always stressed conserving and taking care of the environment we live in. So when this whole sustainability movement started becoming popular, to me it was like, oh? so you mean everyone doesn't already do all this stuff?"

Alyse's family's approach to living green took her to Butte College, where she studies sustainability and journalism. She hopes to one day start a green publishing company. "Last semester for Earth Day, my psychology class hosted a clothing swap, and I ended up with a whole new wardrobe. It was fun, a huge success, and I loved all the great finds I snagged!"

You don't have to be a celebrity or even a teen to make a difference. There are dozens of small changes you can make around your home and school that can help the world become greener. Sesame Street's Kermit the Frog once croaked, "It's not easy being green."

But now being green—or eco-friendly—is easier than ever, and this book will show you how.

Chapter 1

David Chameides (KUH-my-deez) has 10,000 worms in his basement. At the end of 2008, he also had 28.5 pounds of trash, 4 pounds of plastic bags, 69 pounds of paper, 153 glass bottles, 64 plastic bottles and jugs, and 9 pizza boxes. This California resident had been collecting his garbage and **recycling** for one year as an eco-experiment. David wanted to learn firsthand how much trash one person generated. The average American produces 1,600 pounds of garbage a year.

The worms are part of his **compost** bin. After David feeds food scraps to the family dog, Biscuit, and his pet rats, Annie and Sophie, the leftovers, along with waste paper, become food for the worms. The end result of the worms' buffet is compost, or decaying **organic** material, which can then be used in David's garden.

Through David's trash experiment, he hoped to draw attention to the impact each person has on the environment. He also wanted to demonstrate small changes individuals can make to create big impacts on the planet. David's experiment gained him worldwide attention and

CONSUME LESS
SUSTAINABLE DAVE
CONSERVE MORE

was documented on his website at www.365daysoftrash.com. David Chameides, also known as "Sustainable Dave," gave a boost to the growing green living movement.

David helped to increase awareness through his garbage collection. At the end of his yearlong experiment, his garbage was moved to the Connecticut Resources Recovery Authority (CRRA) Trash Museum in Hartford, Connecticut, for others to consider.

David's dog Biscuit

1908 Ford Model T

THE AGE OF AMBIVALENCE

There's a better way than barrels of oil
There's a better way than lumps of coal
There's a better way to work together
Renewable *power, that's our goal*
  —Dan Berggren, "Power from Above"

On his 2006 album *Fresh Territory,* New York folksinger Dan Berggren sings about alternative ways to power the world without causing so much environmental damage. In his song "Power from Above," he sings, "No one owns the wind or sun." He encourages energy consumers to move away from traditional fossil fuels and look for **alternative energy** sources, such as wind and solar energy.

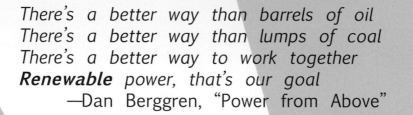

Shoe Cobbler

Pearl Street Electric Lighting Station

Change is not easy. But change is necessary if the United States, and other countries around the world, is going to recover from what some experts have called the Age of **Ambivalence**, a period of time from 1960 to 2000 when customers bought without thinking.

In 1962, ecologist Rachel Carson wrote *Silent Spring*. Her book pointed out the damage caused to the environment by chemicals, especially those used in farming. Her writings stressed how people are just one part of nature, and what sets them apart is their power to change nature—whether for good or ill. The world took notice, and some people began to purposefully change the way they lived. Despite the growing awareness, consumerism increased.

Consumerism in the world has been changing for hundreds of years. Modern machines and factories first took root in the years 1800 to 1860. The shoe cobbler was no longer needed to make shoes. Factories made hundreds of shoes during the same time it would take the cobbler to craft a single pair. Steam was used to power not only machinery but also the railways that moved these goods to other geographical areas.

In 1882, the first street in New York City was illuminated by electric lamps. Electricity found its way out of scientists' laboratories and into the cities. Soon, electricity flowed into the factories and homes of Americans and others around the world. From 1870 through 1914, people experienced a second industrial revolution, this one driven by electricity.

In 1914, attention moved away from production to the battlefields. World War I drained many of the world's resources. Manufacturers turned to **mass production** to aid in the world's recovery. Companies replaced what was used during the war, and then made more products in great quantities.

It was during this same time period that Henry Ford founded two things: a car that the common man could afford, and the assembly line to mass-produce it. Ford introduced his gasoline-powered Model T in 1908.

From 1929 through the 1930s, many families suffered hardships. During this period, called the Great Depression, there was little or nothing to buy, sell, or eat. As World War II began, food, gas, and clothing were **rationed**.

Although World War II restricted much of what consumers could have, the period that followed was rich in technological advancements and material goods. Many families moved away from inner cities and relocated to suburbs and rural areas of the country. They drove longer distances to get to work. They purchased large cars to get there and back.

It was only when the future was considered as a critical component of the present that the environmental movement began. It wasn't a mass movement but a trickle. After Carson's book was published, one person shared his ideas with another, who shared them with yet another. People encouraged others to conserve, reduce, reuse, and recycle. Consumers began to question their throwaway mentality.

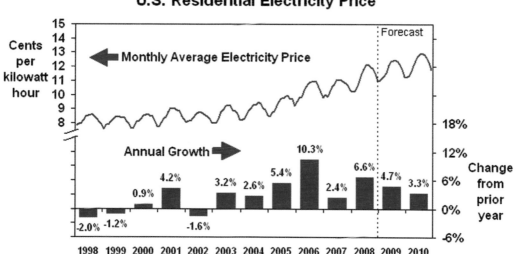

U.S. Residential Electricity Price

The average cost to purchase electricity has risen steadily since 1998. As U.S. residents look to reduce power usage, energy experts project the growth of this utility service to be on the decline.

By 2005, many green efforts were well under way around the world. The top seven environmentally friendly countries were Finland, Norway, Uruguay, Sweden, Iceland, Canada, and Switzerland. Where was the United States?

The United States lags far behind other countries' green efforts. In 2009, ninety-one percent of U.S. employees were commuting to work by car, without any passengers along for the ride. The average European car got 35 miles per gallon of gasoline. The average American car, however, could travel only 20 miles on a gallon of gas. In 2008–2009, the United States experienced an economic crisis. The U.S. government had to financially bail out the country's failing auto industry. In return, U.S. car manufacturers were required to produce more fuel-efficient vehicles.

Meanwhile, Americans have continued to build larger and larger homes. The average U.S. home in 1978 was 1,750 square feet. In 2006, that number jumped to 2,500 square feet, a 43 percent increase in size. Sixty percent of all harvested trees are used to build homes. And larger homes require more natural resources to keep them warm or cool, and more cleaning products to keep them sanitary.

Water is another natural resource. In the United States, the average water consumption is 176 gallons per person per day. Of the countries surveyed by WaterPartners International, only Canada consumed more (209 gallons per person per day). The U.S. government predicted that by 2013, thirty-six states would be challenged by water shortages.

Timothy W. Jones, an anthropologist at the University of Arizona, studied American food habits for ten years,

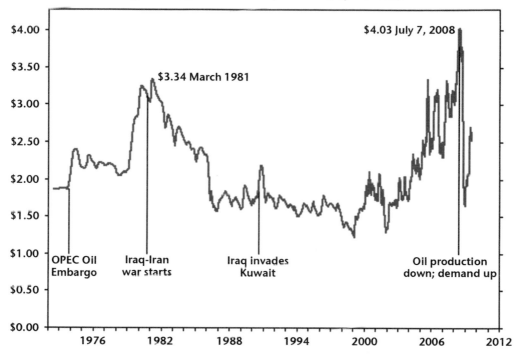

Regular Gasoline Price in Today's Dollars (July 13, 2009)

Each week, the U.S. Department of Energy records and averages gasoline prices around the country. In 2008, Americans were shocked when gasoline prices exceeded $4.00 a gallon. They were forced to take a closer look at their gasoline consumption. As they reduced their gasoline usage, the oil industry responded. With a lower demand, prices fell.

between 1994 and 2004. He learned that 40 to 50 percent of all food grown is never consumed. Jones discovered that the average American family of four people was throwing out almost $600 worth of meat, fruits, and vegetables each year. On a national scale, that equaled $43 billion worth of tossed food, much of which was still good to consume.

On the farmlands of Pennsylvania, Ohio, Indiana, and other states live the Amish. Known as "plain people," they rely little on the services of others. The Amish use horses and buggies for transportation. They grow much of their own food, fertilized by the manure from their horses and cows. They eat produce in season, with the extra "put up"—preserved by canning or other methods—for use during the nongrowing season. They make their own clothing, which is designed for easy alterations as they grow. They do not rely on outside electricity to run their homes or farms. The Amish have been living green since their formation in Switzerland in the late 1700s.

Americans were purchasing more of everything—from fuel for their gas-guzzling cars to multiple television sets, computers, video games, appliances, and pieces of clothing. They moved away from fixing what was broken or donating unwanted items and toward tossing them away. America became a disposable society.

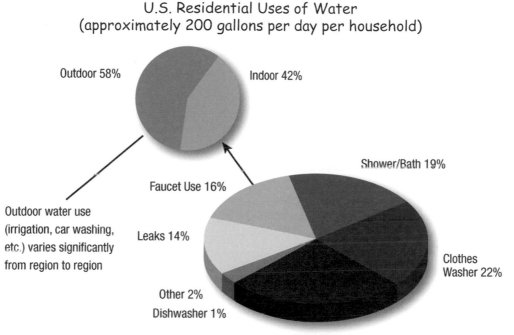

U.S. Residential Uses of Water
(approximately 200 gallons per day per household)

Outdoor 58%

Indoor 42%

Shower/Bath 19%

Faucet Use 16%

Outdoor water use
(irrigation, car washing,
etc.) varies significantly
from region to region

Leaks 14%

Clothes
Washer 22%

Other 2%

Dishwasher 1%

Toilet 26%

Americans consume more water than most other countries. Although the majority of our water is used for cleanliness, 14 percent is lost through leaks in the system that brings water to our homes, and in our homes themselves through leaky faucets and faulty plumbing.

With greater environmental awareness, Americans entered a period of transition. They began moving from the Age of Ambivalence to the Age of Living Green. They were finding that even the smallest individual changes, when multiplied by the number of people making those changes, can make a huge difference in the world.

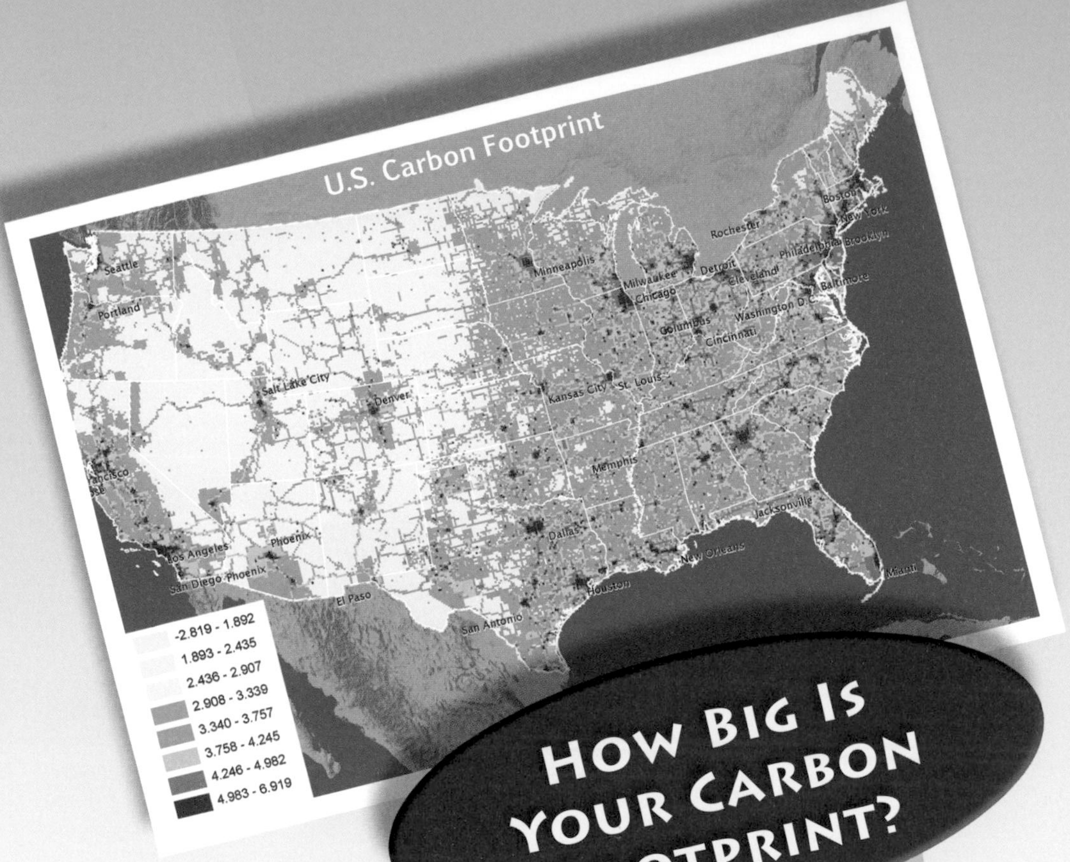

Seattle
Portland
San Francisco Bay
Los Angeles
San Diego Phoenix
Phoenix
El Paso
San Antonio
Salt Lake City
Denver
Kansas City   St. Louis
Minneapolis
Milwaukee   Detroit   Cleveland
Chicago
Columbus   Washington D.C.
Cincinnati
Memphis
Dallas
Houston   New Orleans
Jacksonville
Miami
Rochester   Boston   New York   Brooklyn
Philadelphia   Baltimore

-2.819 - 1.892
1.893 - 2.435
2.436 - 2.907
2.908 - 3.339
3.340 - 3.757
3.758 - 4.245
4.246 - 4.982
4.983 - 6.919

HOW BIG IS YOUR CARBON FOOTPRINT?

Everything you do has an impact on the environment. With each step you take throughout the day, you leave behind what scientists call your carbon footprint.

Your carbon footprint is the measurement of how much carbon dioxide and other gases you produce, whether directly or indirectly. For example, one ton of carbon dioxide (CO_2) is released when an airplane flies 5,000 miles. Even if you aren't a passenger on the plane, perhaps a package you've mailed or are having delivered to you accounts for a small percentage of that pollution. One ton of CO_2 is released when you and your family travel 2,500 miles in a medium-sized

At the Tracy Biomass Plant in California, a truck unloads wood chips that will be used to fuel the plant

Wairakei Geothermal Power Station

car. Carbon dioxide is also produced when electricity is generated in a coal-burning power plant.

Carbon dioxide is just one gas that is released into the environment. Other greenhouse gases include methane and nitrous oxide. Your actions may not emit these gases directly, but the choices you make each day do. One-fifth of all greenhouse gas emissions come from livestock. The dairy cattle that supply milk and the animals that are processed for meat all produce methane. To reduce their carbon footprint, many people choose not to eat meat or dairy.

Some scientists believe that these greenhouse gases are the primary cause of global changes. They believe that by reducing our individual carbon footprints, we can reduce the impact we have on the world.

The United States has one of the largest carbon footprints. The average American emits 27 tons of CO_2 each year. The average world citizen, however, emits

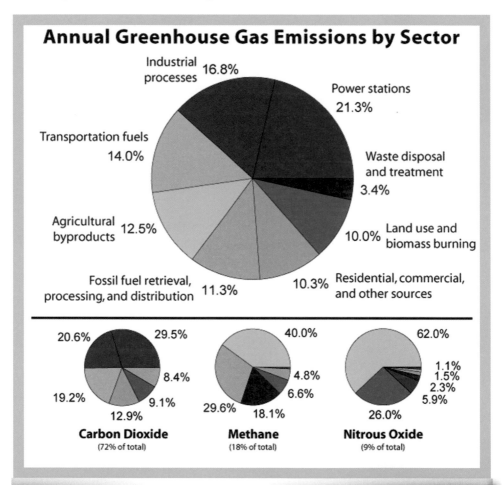

Annual Greenhouse Gas Emissions by Sector

Industrial processes 16.8%

Power stations 21.3%

Transportation fuels 14.0%

Waste disposal and treatment 3.4%

Agricultural byproducts 12.5%

Land use and biomass burning 10.0%

Fossil fuel retrieval, processing, and distribution 11.3%

Residential, commercial, and other sources 10.3%

Carbon Dioxide (72% of total)
20.6% 29.5% 8.4% 9.1% 12.9% 19.2%

Methane (18% of total)
40.0% 4.8% 6.6% 18.1% 29.6%

Nitrous Oxide (9% of total)
62.0% 1.1% 1.5% 2.3% 5.9% 26.0%

Although only 12.5 percent of all greenhouse gases are produced by the agricultural sector, it is the largest contributor of both methane and nitrous oxide. Individuals who choose to limit meat and dairy consumption cite the gas production as one of their reasons for making this personal choice.

only 5.5 tons. Much of each footprint is filled by electrical generation to satisfy energy consumption.

In the United States, the energy used to create electricity mostly comes from (in order of percent generated) coal, **nuclear** power plants, natural gas, **hydroelectric** dams, and petroleum. Coal, natural gas, and petroleum are **nonrenewable** natural resources. It can take millions of years for the earth to replenish these resources. As these fossil fuels burn, they release CO_2.

France generates most of its electricity using nuclear power, which harnesses the power of atoms to create energy. Germany, however, is in the process of shutting down its nuclear plants. In 2008, the United States had 104 active nuclear reactors, generating almost 20 percent of the nation's electricity. Although nuclear power plants emit few greenhouse gases, opponents of nuclear power question its safety, especially in the storage and disposal of **radioactive waste**.

Hydroelectric power captures the power of water to generate energy. Over 2,000 hydroelectric plants operate in the United States, producing almost 50 percent of the nation's renewable energy.

Scientists are working diligently to bring other sources of energy to consumers, including solar energy, wind power, **biomass** (burning of natural materials, like trees, plants, and garbage), and **geothermal** power (heat from inside the earth).

The use of alternative fuels may help to reduce carbon emissions. In the meantime, individuals can try to use less electricity.

Energy Changes You and Your Family Can Make

• Each year, Americans spend $4 billion on electricity that they are not even using, such as for computers, chargers, and appliances left plugged in. Known as phantom electricity, this nonuse accounts for 5 to 15 percent of a home's monthly electric bill, and it is responsible for releasing 27 tons of carbon dioxide (CO_2) into the atmosphere. To avoid using phantom electricity, turn off the lights when you leave a room. Turn the TV set off when no one is watching it. And unplug appliances, computers, and recharging devices when they're not in use.

• Replace standard lightbulbs with energy-efficient lightbulbs. These bulbs take longer to warm up than conventional bulbs, and they may not be as bright, but they use 75 percent less electricity and last ten times longer. Handle these bulbs carefully. They contain mercury, a toxic metal.

• Lower the temperature setting on the water heater. Setting your water temperature to 120°F is ideal. For each 10 degrees a family lowers the dial on its water heater, 3 to 5 percent can be saved on its electric bill. Then, give your water heater a warm, winter coat of a blanket or insulation to keep the heat in. (You can also set the water heater on a timer, so that you're not heating water when you're less likely to use it.)

Water Heater

Thermostat

• Close the curtains or blinds on hot summer days to keep out the heat of the sun.

• Turn down heat. Turn up air conditioners. (Or turn them off and open the windows!) When you leave the house, turn the heat down or air conditioner up even more. If you can't remember to do this, install programmable thermostats, which will adjust the temperature of the house automatically.

Nonrenewable resources are also used to power our vehicles. Most U.S. families own one or more cars, and the car is their first choice in transportation. Most American cars are fueled by gasoline or diesel fuel, which are petroleum products. For decades, engineers have been working on cars that use alternative fuels. In fact, the first cars built were electric, but they were not as popular as gasoline-powered cars. By the 1970s,

• Some families will heat their homes with wood. Even though burning wood releases CO_2, some people say that the amount produced by burning the tree is exactly the same as the amount the tree absorbed from the atmosphere during its lifetime. While this exchange rate is debatable, it is important to research the choice of wood burners well. Pollution rates vary for fireplaces, wood-burning stoves, and furnaces.

• Wash clothes in cold water, and run the washing machine and dishwasher only when they are full.

• Use a drying rack to air dry your clothes.

• Select renewable energy sources, such as wind or solar power, if they are available from your energy supplier.

• Replace worn-out appliances with Energy-Star appliances, which are more energy efficient. Depending on the type of appliance you choose, your family may qualify for tax credits.

electric cars were making a comeback, but consumers just weren't buying them. In 2000, Toyota introduced the gasoline-electric hybrid called the Prius. Consumers bought thousands of them. Now there are many alternative-fuel cars on the market.

Some cars are purely electric. Depending on how their batteries are charged, they may not be the best environmental choice for transportation. Some consumers

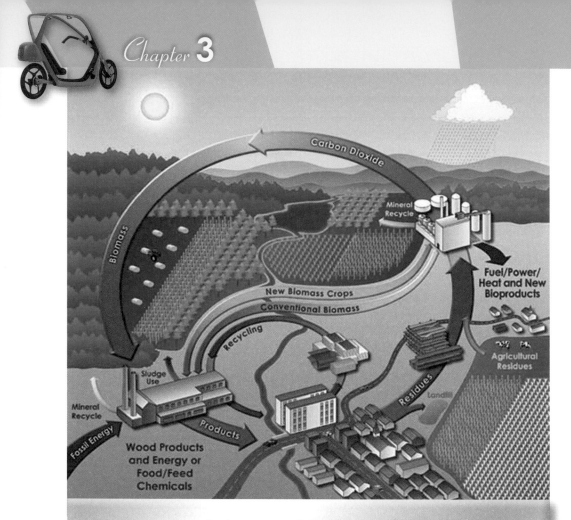

Scientists are exploring more elaborate uses for biomass energy. Industrial power plants can burn vegetation to produce energy. As CO_2 is emitted in the burning process, growing plants can use the gas for making their food.

charge their cars by plugging into their home electrical systems, which may be supplied by carbon dioxide-producing energy sources. Others, however, have solar chargers, which have less impact on the environment. As electric car networks and eco-friendly recharging stations become more readily available, these cars may be viewed as a better consumer option.

Transportation Changes You and Your Family Can Make

• Challenge your family to use the car less and other transportation options more. Use public transportation whenever possible. Besides reducing the number of vehicles on the road, many public transportation systems use buses and trains that run on alternative fuels.

• Combine errands into fewer trips. Carpool with friends and neighbors.

• Schedule regular car maintenance appointments to check the air filter, maintain tire pressure, and change the oil.

• Do not allow your car to idle.

• Walk or bike whenever possible. You may also want to roller-skate or ride your scooter. If you do, use walk or bike paths and always observe safety rules, including wearing a helmet.

• The next time your family is in the market for a new car, ask them to consider purchasing a hybrid or more fuel-efficient vehicle. If your family owns a diesel car, ask them to think about converting it to run on biodiesel fuel.

FAMILY CHANGES

Everyone has to eat food and drink water to survive. Maintaining a clean household is an additional key to survival. After all, trash and germs breed diseases. Modern products have made obtaining food, water, and cleanliness easier and more convenient. Now people realize they can have their necessities at a much lower environmental cost, but without loss of convenience.

Like energy, our food can come from both traditional and nontraditional sources. Grocery stores are jam-packed with food from all over the globe. In the United States, most food travels 1,500 to 2,500 miles before it reaches the kitchen table. Because consumers now realize that the most nutritious and freshest food comes from local farmers, they are flocking to food

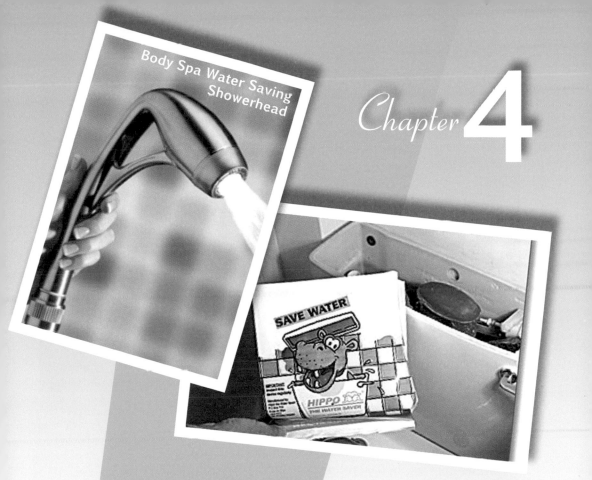

Body Spa Water Saving Showerhead

sources in their own backyards. These same green consumers are also searching for new restaurants offering locally grown and purchased (within 50 miles) food. Called **locavores**, these consumers are no longer satisfied with tomatoes picked before they are ripe and shipped to stores thousands of miles away.

Because so many people want to buy locally, more and more farmers markets are opening throughout the country. According to the U.S. Department of Agriculture, in 2008, there were almost 4,700 operating farmers markets. That is a 6.8 percent growth in farmers markets from 2006.

Eco-savvy consumers are also shopping at health food stores and **cooperatives**, where food is fresh, usually organic, and may cost less than traditional

Because of chemicals that may be left behind on conventionally grown foods, many scientists and nutritionists recommend that you purchase these ten foods from organic suppliers: strawberries, bell peppers, spinach, cherries, peaches, cantaloupe, celery, apples, apricots, and green beans.

stores. Recognizing the demand for "green" food, many big-chain grocery stores have built small health food centers within their larger businesses.

Some consumers are buying into the local produce movement by purchasing shares of CSAs, or **Community Supported Agriculture** programs. As members of a CSA, families receive weekly bags of locally grown and in-season produce. They may also choose to work on the farm as part of their payment.

Food isn't the only consumable product. Anything you can "use up," such as paper and health-care products, are also considered consumables.

Food and Other Consumable Product Changes You and Your Family Can Make

• Eat meatless meals at least one day each week. Look for good vegetarian protein sources, such as beans and soy products, to meet your nutritional needs. Reducing meat consumption will reduce not only methane production, but water usage as well. Some agricultural experts estimate that it takes 25 gallons of water to produce a pound of wheat and 2,500 pounds of water to produce a pound of meat.

• Savor leftovers. Freeze leftover soup, chili, stews, and sauces for future meals.

• Purchase recycled paper products, including toilet tissue and printer paper.

• Use both sides of your computer paper.

• Wrap presents in old comic pages from the newspaper, or make your own wrapping paper from old paper bags.

• Borrow books from the library rather than purchasing them.

• Buy local, organic produce.

• Use natural health care products that don't contain harmful ingredients that you could inhale or absorb into your body. Look for environmentally friendly pet care products, too.

• Purchase natural home cleaning products, or to save money, make your own environmentally friendly cleaning products. For recipes, visit Eartheasy at http://www. eartheasy.com/live_nontoxic_solutions.htm.

• Pack your lunch in reusable containers instead of plastic bags and wrap. You can even buy washable fabric containers that are FDA Approved for holding food.

• In the near future, you may see disposable water bottles made of recycled paper. Even better, use environmentally friendly reusable water bottles.

Water distribution engineers are exploring more extensive water treatment systems, where yesterday's sewage can become today's drinking water. Someday, untreated water, from toilets, showers, and washing machines, may flow into one end of the treatment plant, and treated water may flow out the other, through the distribution system, and into the consumer's glass. You, too, can be a water engineer, by using a barrel to collect rainwater for non-drinking purposes.

Earth has a limited supply of fresh water. Most of it comes from surface water (lakes, reservoirs, streams, rivers) and groundwater (wells). Regional water systems treat and distribute water to their consumers.

Eco-savvy consumers are looking for ways to reduce their water usage. They may collect rainwater and dirty bathwater to wash their dog or for use in their gardens. What can you and your family do to reduce your water consumption?

For each minute the water is left running while brushing teeth, up to two gallons of water flows down the drain. With each flush of a conventional toilet, seven gallons of water travels to the wastewater treatment plant or home septic system.

Water Usage Changes You and Your Family Can Make

- Turn off the water while brushing your teeth.
- Limit your shower time. (Sing a song in the shower. When the song is done, so are you!)
- Install low-flow toilets, or create a water dam inside the toilet tank to reduce the water needed for each flush. Be sure there is still enough water to wash it all down with one flush, however.
- Repair leaky faucets.
- Wash your car at the car wash. Car-wash water is captured and recycled, so cleaning products are not washed into drains or the ground, and the water can be used again.
- Let your grass grow! Longer grass develops deeper roots and stores more moisture in its blades. The ideal length of your grass will depend on the type of grass you have planted.
- Include native plants in your landscape. Because these plants grow naturally in your area, they require less water.
- Convert some of your grass area into a rock garden.

Since the late 1900s, Americans have come a long way in their trash disposal and recycling efforts. It wasn't too long ago that all trash was collected and sent to the trash dump or floated out to sea. Today, most families separate trash from recyclable items and dispose of them properly. Some states require deposits on bottles and cans that can be recycled. This money is returned to the consumer at recycling processing centers.

Even with these efforts, in 2008, the U.S. Environmental Protection Agency (EPA) estimated that the average American generates about 1,600 pounds of trash annually. At least half of this trash ends up in landfills. With the U.S. population in 2008 exceeding 305 million people, residents of the United States are tossing 242,400,000,000 (242 *billion*) pounds of garbage away each year. Much of it is packaging materials.

Other contributors to trash heaps are food and yard waste, much of which could be composted. Individuals have been encouraged to compost, but many people don't have the space to do this efficiently. Perhaps one day, there will be community compost bins where food and yard waste can be collected, consumed by worms, and made into usable garden soil.

Today's trash can be tomorrow's treasure. In 2009, about 30 percent of all household trash in the United States was sent to recycling plants. Some experts, however, believe this number could be as high as 70 percent. What can you do to increase this number?

In 2009, the Australian town of Bundanoon outlawed bottled water. Environmentalists calculate that it takes twice as much water to produce the plastic bottle that holds the water that buyers consume. Many of those bottles are tossed rather than recycled.

For one week, collect the plastic water bottles that you, your classmates, and their families use. Add them up! Then, multiply this number by the number of classrooms in your school. That's an estimate of the number of bottles your "school family" is consuming each week. Double the number and you'll discover how much water was needed to produce those bottles. What can you do to reduce this number?

To encourage consumers to make wiser purchasing choices, recycle more, and reduce their trash load, some communities are turning to Pay-as-You-Throw programs. Consumers are charged per bag or per pound of trash.

Sustainable Dave (from Chapter 1) encourages young readers to "keep a list of all your trash for a week. You'll be surprised at how much it is and want to make changes."

The United States, in step with other green countries, is making progress in reducing the size of the millions of carbon footprints its residents are leaving behind. Whether it's making wiser energy choices, walking more and driving less, purchasing food from local sources, or reducing, reusing, and recycling, every wise environmental choice makes a difference in the health of the planet.

Trash Changes You and Your Family Can Make

• Start a compost bin. (Don't forget the worms!) Any food waste that comes from plants, eggshells, shells from crabs and clams, and tea bags and coffee grounds can be composted. (Do not compost meat, bones, dairy products, or cat litter.)

• Separate all recyclables from regular trash. Dispose of hazardous waste properly.

• Ask companies to stop sending you junk mail.

• To reduce packaging, buy in bulk. (But don't buy more than you can use.) Buy fewer single-serving packages, such as beverage bottles.

• Sell or donate unwanted items rather than throwing them away. You could give your used magazines to hospitals, nursing homes, senior centers, doctors' offices, day care centers, after-school programs, and other facilities; or give your used toys and clothing to those who need them.

CANVAS
The New
Plastic

• Buy and use reusable canvas bags for your shopping. Or bring your own plastic or paper bags to the store.

• Instead of using paper towels, use a mop or washable rag to wipe up spills. Use cloth towels for drying your hands.

• Refill or recycle used ink cartridges, or donate them to a cause that collects them.

• Donate old cell phones to organizations that can use them.

Electric Plug-in Unit

EVERY CHANGE MAKES A DIFFERENCE

Living green isn't an all-or-nothing proposition. With every change you make, your carbon footprint gets a little smaller, and the earth gets a little greener.

What if you told just three people about green living? And what if each of them told three more people? And what if those people told three more people? Your green knowledge can change the lives of 27 people or more! Your green knowledge can change the earth.

By making little changes, not only can you and your family reduce your impact on the earth, but you can also reduce your **utility** bills. Ask your parents to share the utility bills with you each month. As you

Governor Arnold Schwarzenegger inspects solar panels

make changes, watch how those changes improve the family budget.

In January 2009, the world watched as green-thinker Barack Obama took the oath for U.S. president. The bicycle-riding president planned to create five million "green collar" jobs during his presidency. These jobs would focus on renewable energy sources, such as wind and solar power. The president also planned to convert the White House fleet of cars to plug-in **hybrid vehicles** before the end of his first year in office and give substantial tax incentives to Americans who purchase environmentally friendly cars.

Film star and **environmentalist** Leonardo DiCaprio travels on commercial planes instead of private jets.

Jasmine Saville and her family of Wales, United Kingdom, wanted to live in harmony with nature. They created an eco-home out of mud, sticks, stone, and straw. The house is heated by a woodstove, and food in the fridge is cooled by underground air. Natural light filters in through skylights, and water flows via gravity from an uphill spring. They don't need to flush the toilet. It goes to a compost pit!

He installed solar panels on his house to reduce his dependency on the electric company for his power. In 2007, he cowrote and co-produced a documentary film called *The Eleventh Hour*. It explained the problem of global warming and encouraged the public to get involved.

Terminator movie star and California Governor Arnold Schwarzenegger is an advocate of solar power. As governor, he signed groundbreaking green legislation. He has also supported Tesla Motor Corporation, which builds electric sports cars in his state.

One of the leading celebrity environmentalists, however, is Ed Begley Jr. The Academy Award–winning star rides his bicycle to Hollywood events. His home is powered by solar energy. He drives an electric car and is actively involved in several environmental organizations, such as Earth Cinema Circle, Thoreau Institute, and Environmental Research Foundation. To help others help the environment, he has created a line of environmentally friendly cleaning products called Begley's Best. He also hosts a cable TV show called *Living with Ed.* It shows all the green changes he's made at home and how they work.

Everyday citizens are also making a difference. We met Dave Chameides in Chapter 1. Dave does more than collect garbage, write blogs to spread environmental awareness, and feed composting worms. When he became a father, he decided it was time to make a difference. He admits that he used to drive a gas-guzzling four-wheel-drive truck, but he wanted to set an example for his daughters by making changes in his transportation choices. Now he drives a car powered by vegetable oil. A solar cell on his family's roof generates most of the power they need to run their home. A solar tube in the hallway allows daylight to illuminate much of their home during the day.

The environmentalist is also an author. His book, *365 Days of Solutions*, was scheduled for release in 2010.

World citizens are trying to make the earth a greener planet. In Copenhagen, Denmark, instead of driving cars,

36 percent of residents bike to work or school. In Ireland, after a tax was placed on plastic bags, residents reduced their plastic bag usage by 90 percent.

Denmark and Israel were the first to announce their plans to build the world's first electric car networks, where cars powered by batteries, and not gasoline, can recharge along their travel routes. Denmark's network will be powered by wind energy. In 2008, Australia announced plans to create a similar network.

For President Barack Obama and his family, green living is everyday living. In the Kenilworth Aquatic Gardens in Washington, D.C., the president helped to plant a tree as part of the greening efforts of the Student Conservation Association, a national organization working in all 50 states to protect and restore green spaces.

For Disney, the key to green success is empowerment. Disney stars Miley Cyrus, Selena Gomez, the Jonas Brothers, and Demi Lovato have joined other young stars as part of Disney's Friends for Change: Project Green. With the focus on climate, water, waste, and habitats, the program encourages green-minded kids to investigate green living, make a difference, and help decide how $1 million in Disney donations will be used to make the planet greener.

Countries are made up of individual citizens, like you. You can make a difference. You can change the world. Before you eat that fast-food burger, toss your plastic water bottle into the garbage, leave a room without turning off the light or television, or allow the water to run while you brush your teeth, stop and think. What change do you want to see in the world? What role can you play in making it happen?

Try This!

Things You Will Need
A cardboard box (opened)
Nature pictures from old magazines
Scissors
Pencil
Ruler
Glue

1. Cut a rectangle out of your box.
2. Place the rectangle on the picture you want to use. Trace the rectangle.
3. Cut out your picture.
4. Apply glue to the back of your picture.
5. Adhere the picture to the printed side of the cardboard.
6. Carefully fold the cardboard in half.
7. Place the folded cardboard with the "fold" edge to the left.
8. With your ruler, draw two parallel lines, starting at the fold and extending about one inch. You can use the width of your ruler as the distance between the lines. These lines can be at the bottom (as shown), the top, or in the middle of the fold, depending on your picture.
9. Carefully cut along the two parallel lines.
10. Open the card and carefully push the formed rectangle through to the inside, making new folds, to create a pop-up cube shape.
11. Glue another picture to a small piece of cardboard. This will become the pop-up part of the card.
12. Attach the new picture to the front of the pop-up cube as shown.
13. Add a message to your card and send it to a friend (or to someone who could use a pop-up smile).

Historical Timeline

1832–1839	Robert Anderson of Scotland invents the electric carriage.
1861	French inventor Auguste Mouchout develops a steam engine that is powered entirely by the sun.
1879	Thomas Edison invents the electric lightbulb.
1891	William Morrison builds the first successful electric automobile in the United States.
1900	At the World's Fair in Paris, France, a diesel engine operates on peanut oil. Electric cars hit the streets of major American cities.
1908	Henry Ford unveils the affordable Model T.
1937	Belgian scientist G. Chavanne is granted a patent for the transformation of vegetable oil into fuel. It is the first biodiesel substance.
1942	Work is completed on the Grand Coulee Power Station in Washington State, the largest U.S. hydropower plant ever constructed.
1953	Bell Laboratories (now AT&T Labs) scientists Gerald Pearson, Daryl Chapin, and Calvin Fuller develop the first silicon solar cell. It can generate a measurable electric current.
1957	The first plastic sandwich bag is made.
1962	*Silent Spring* by Rachel Carson is published.
1972	Funded by the U.S. Environmental Protection Agency (EPA), Victor Wouk builds the first full-size hybrid vehicle using a 1972 Buick Skylark.
1976	The EPA cancels the Clean Car Incentive Program. General Electric scientist Edward Hammer invents the first compact fluorescent lightbulb. It is not produced, however, because of high manufacturing costs.
1977	The Department of Energy is created. The Solar Energy Research Institute (later called National Renewable Energy Laboratory) is founded in Golden, Colorado. Grocery stores begin to offer the choice of plastic or paper bags.
1979	The worst nuclear disaster in U.S. history occurs at Three Mile Island Nuclear Plant in Middletown, Pennsylvania.
1980	The Sustainable Buildings Industry Council (SBIC) is founded by building trade associations to focus on the design and construction of "greener" homes. U.S. Windpower installs the world's first wind farm.
1987	National Appliance Energy Conservation Act is enacted to bring energy-efficient standards to homes. The United Nation's World Commission on the Environment and Development defines "sustainable development" as that which "meets the needs of the present without compromising the ability of future generations to meet their own needs."
1993	President Bill Clinton announces plans to make the White House "a model for efficiency and waste reduction."
1997	The Kyoto Protocol is adopted by 87 countries, including the United States, with the goal to reduce global carbon emissions. Toyota unveils the Prius in Japan.
1999	The U.S. President's Council on Sustainable Development recommends 140 actions to improve the nation's environment.
2001	The United States withdraws from the Kyoto Protocol, citing economic reasons.
2006	*An Inconvenient Truth*, Al Gore's documentary about global warming, is released.
2008	David Chameides collects his garbage for one year and blogs about the experience on http://www.365daysoftrash.blogspot.com. Denmark and Israel announce plans to build networks for charging electric cars.
2009	U.S. President Barack Obama designates dollars to help the country reduce its carbon footprint while improving a green-collar economy.

Further Reading

Amsel, Sheri. *Everything Kids' Environment Book: Learn How You Can Help the Environment by Getting Involved at School, at Home, or at Play.* Cincinnati, OH: Adams Media, 2007.

Gershon, David. *Journey for the Planet: A Kid's Five-Week Adventure to Create an Earth-friendly Life.* Woodstock, NY: Empowerment Institute, 2007.

Olien, Rebecca. *Kids Care!: 75 Ways to Make a Difference for People, Animals and the Environment.* Nashville, TN: Williamson Books, 2007.

Savedge, Jenn. *The Green Parent: A Kid-friendly Guide to Earth-friendly Living.* Seattle: Kedzie Press LLC, 2008.

Works Consulted

This book is based on the author's interviews with David Chameides on December 31, 2008, and with Alyse Lui on January 3, 2009, and on e-mail correspondence with Dan Berggren in December 2008. She also used the following sources:

Bach, David. *Go Green, Live Rich: 50 Simple Ways to Save the Earth.* New York: Broadway Books, 2008.

Berggren, Dan. *Fresh Territory*: "Power from Above" http://www.berggrenfolk.com/albums_details.cfm?aid=25

"Calif. Man Lives With His Own Garbage for a Year." CBS, December 29, 2008. http://cbs5.com/consumer/man.keeps.trash.2.896291.html

Chameides, David. *365 Days of Trash.* http://365daysoftrash.blogspot.com/

Cooper, Max. "Plan for Electric Car Network." *The Age,* October 23, 2008. http://www.theage.com.au/national/plan-for-electric-car-network-20081023-56zz.html?page=-1

"Denmark's Electric Car Network Will Use Wind Power." Environmental News Service, April 1, 2008. http://www.ens-newswire.com/ens/apr2008/2008-04-01-02.asp

Ed Begley, Jr. http://www.edbegley.com/environment/

Energy Information Administration. Official Energy Statistics from the U.S. Government http://www.eia.doe.gov/

Food from the 'Hood. http://www.certnyc.org/ffth.html

Green Teen Community Gardening Program. http://www.greenteen.org/index.htm

Lean, Geoffrey, and Leonard Doyle. "Obama's Green Jobs Revolution." *The Independent,* November 2, 2008. http://www.independent.co.uk/news/world/americas/obamas-green-jobs-revolution-984631.html

Lous, Renee. *Easy Green Living: The Ultimate Guide to Simple, Eco-friendly Choices for You and Your Family.* New York: Rodale Inc., 2008.

McDilda, Diane Gow. *The Everything Green Living Book.* Avon, Massachusetts: Adams Media, 2007.

Melville, Kate. "U.S. Throws Away Half Its Food." *Science a Go Go,* November 24, 2004. http://www.scienceagogo.com/news/20041024002637data_trunc_sys.shtml

The Pros and Cons of Compact Fluorescent Lightbulbs (CFLs). http://greennature.com/article256.html

Schuyt, Ian. *The Top 7 Environmentally Friendly Countries.* January 26, 2007. http://www.aboutmyplanet.com/environment/the-top-7-environmentally-friendly-countries/

Tilden, Tommi Lewis. "Hollywood's Green Teen Scene." *The Daily Green,* September 11, 2007. http://www.thedailygreen.com/living-green/blogs/celebrities/6256

Trask, Crissy. *It's Easy Being Green: A Handbook for Earth-friendly Living.* Salt Lake City: Gibbs Smith, 2006.

Uliano, Sophie. *Gorgeously Green: 8 Simple Steps to an Earth-friendly Life.* New York: Collins, 2008.

U.S. Census Bureau. http://www.census.gov/

USDA Wholesale and Farmers Markets: Farmers Market Growth. http://www.ams.usda.gov/AMSv1.0/ams.fetchTemplateData.do?template=TemplateS&navID=WholesaleandFarmersMarkets&leftNav=WholesaleandFarmersMarkets&page=WFMFarmersMarketGrowth&description=Farmers%20Market%20Growth&acct=frmrdirmkt

Waste Partners International: Use of Water Worldwide. http://www.peacecorps.gov/wws/educators/enrichment/africa/lessons/HSgeog01/Hsgeog01sup01.pdf

On the Internet

Environmental Kids Club
    http://www.epa.gov/kids/
The Greens
    http://www.meetthegreens.org/
Ranger Rick's Green Zone
    http://www.nwf.org/rrgreenzone/Default.aspx
Recycle City
    http://www.epa.gov/recyclecity/

Glossary

alternative (ahl-TER-nuh-tiv) **energy**—An environmentally friendly source of energy that is not often used, such as solar or wind power.

ambivalence (am-BIH-vuh-lunts)—Not making a decision or taking a side.

biodiesel (BY-oh-dee-sul)—Fuel made from used vegetable oil, usually from restaurant fryers.

biomass (BY-oh-mass)—Plant material and animal waste that can be burned as fuel.

Community Supported Agriculture (CSA) (kun-MYOO-nih-tee suh-por-ted AG-rih-kul-chur)—A farm program in which members can purchase shares of the farm's activities and in return receive weekly produce during the growing season.

compost (KOM-pohst)—Organic waste that breaks down into soil.

cooperative (koh-AH-pruh-tiv)—A group of people who buy in bulk at lower prices than they could buy individually, and then share their purchases.

eco-entrepreneurs (eh-koh-on-truh-pruh-NOORS), or **eco-preneurs**—People who start businesses that help the environment.

eco-friendly (eh-koh-FREND-lee)—Goods and services that pose little or no harm on the environment.

environmentalist (en-vy-run-MEN-tuh-list)—A person who protects the earth through work, actions, or lifestyle.

fossil fuels—Energy sources such as coal, oil, and natural gas that formed in the earth from plant and animal remains.

geothermal (jee-oh-THER-mul)—Heat from within the earth.

green living—A lifestyle choice that puts the earth first.

hybrid vehicles—Cars and trucks that run on a combination of an engine (such as one that is gasoline-powered) and a motor (such as one that is electric-powered).

hydroelectric (hy-droh-ee-LEK-trik)—Electricity generated by water energy.

locavore (LOH-kuh-voor)—An individual who chooses to consume food that is grown locally, usually within a specific mile radius.

mass production—Making goods in large quantities, usually with machinery.

nonrenewable (non-ree-NOO-uh-bul) **energy**—Energy sources that once used cannot be replaced.

nuclear (NOO-klee-ur)—Power or energy released by atomic reactions.

organic (or-GAA-nik)—Made from plants or animals that contain carbon.

radioactive (ray-dee-oh-AK-tiv) **waste**—A harmful by-product of nuclear reactions.

ration (RAA-shun)—To limit the amount of food and other materials that can be distributed.

recycling (ree-SY-kling)—Turning old material into usable raw goods.

renewable (ree-NOO-uh-bul) **energy**—Energy resources, such as the wind and the sun, that can produce power without being depleted.

sustainable (sus-TAYN-uh-bul) **living**—A lifestyle that does not damage the earth.

toxic (TOK-sik)—Poisonous.

utility (yoo-TIL-ih-tee)—A company that supplies electricity, water, or other services to consumers.

Index

About the AUTHOR

Carol Parenzan Smalley grew up in the shadows of Pennsylvania's Three Mile Island Nuclear Power Plant, the scene of an accidental partial reactor meltdown in 1979. Some of her relatives worked in coal mines. Her family stopped at farm stands along Amish backcountry roads near Lancaster, Pennsylvania, to buy their produce.

Today, she lives with her family in a log cabin in the Adirondack Mountains of upstate New York. She tries to reduce her carbon footprint by buying local organic food, using natural home-care and beauty products, purchasing previously loved clothing for her family, borrowing books from the library, and using cat litter made from recycled newspaper. She received a degree in environmental engineering, with a focus on water resources, from the Pennsylvania State University. Visit her website at www.CarolSmalley.com.